ABCs of Easter

Story and Art by Patricia Reeder Eubank

ideals children's books.
Nashville, Tennessee

ISBN-13: 978-0-8249-5617-2

Published by Ideals Children's Books
An imprint of Ideals Publications
A Guideposts Company
Nashville, Tennessee
www.idealsbooks.com

For William, who is such a
beautiful, imaginative cinematographer
and artist with a never-ending, creative
intelligence; who has such warmth
and kindness, enjoys life tremendously,
and is so much fun to be with; and
who especially loves brown Newfies.

Color separations by Precision Color
Graphics, Franklin, Wisconsin
Printed and bound in the USA

Library of Congress CIP data on file

Designed by Eve DeGrie

Worz_Jan10_1

You can visit Patti Eubank online
at www.patriciaeubank.com

When Easter Day draws near,
Three fuzzy bunnies read and peer
At the ABCs of springtime fun
And Easter joy for everyone.

A

A is for airy, azure blue skies,
amethyst azaleas,
and soft April showers.

B is for bright-
ribboned bonnets,
bold, busy bunnies,
and baskets of flowers.

B

C is for creamy milk chocolate,
cottontail candies,
and cute, cuddly chicks
the color of cheese.

D is for dear, downy ducks,
dazzling dyed eggs,
and dancing in dresses
by dogwood trees.

E

E is for elegant baskets,
exciting egg hunts,
and little hands eager
to paint Easter eggs.

F is for fragrant, fresh flowers
and frolicking friends
with four furry legs.

F

G is for gathering garlands
in a glorious garden
of glistening green grasses.

H is for hundreds of hyacinths
and hopping hares
hiding heaps of eggs
for lads and lasses.

H

I is for indigo irises
and inspired Easter invitations
to friends near and far.

J is for jumbo jawbreakers
and jolly-colored jellybeans
jumbled in a jar.

K

K is for kissing
precious new kittens
and a kaleidoscope sky
of colorful kites.

L is for luminous lilies,
lavender lilacs,
and lunching lambs taking
lazy little bites.

L

M

M is for morning glories,
munching marshmallow treats,
and humming along
to Easter melodies.

N is for newly hatched robins
napping in nests
nestled high in the trees.

O

O is for owlets eyeing
oval-shaped eggs
and oodles of fun under
oak trees with knots.

P is for parades with
pink and purple parasols
and prim and proper people
in pastels and polka dots.

Q

Q is for quarrelsome,
quacking geese
quizzically pecking
at quilts with their bills.

R is for egg rolls
and rambunctious races,
roaring with laughter,
and rolling down hills.

R

S

S is for steeples,
bright stained-glass windows,
and sweet sugar eggs,
so softly spun.

T is for treetops,
twittering bird tunes,
and tangles of tulips
tilting up toward the sun.

U

U is for uncovering
Ukrainian eggs
with their unique designs
and ultra-bright hues.

V is for verdant valleys
filled with vivid violets,
from vernal pinks
to vibrant blues.

W

W is for white, fluffy clouds and web-footed ducklings that wiggle and waddle when bidden.

X marks the spot where the Easter eggs are hidden!

Y is for yellow daffodils
dotting the yard
to signal the start
of springtime each year.

Z is for the buzzing of bees
zipping through the air
when Easter's end is near.